Sleepytime for Zoo Animals

by Caroline Arnold   photographs by Richard Hewett

Carolrhoda Books, Inc./Minneapolis

When you are tired,
what do you do?
You take a nap.
Zoo animals need
to rest, too.

orangutan

A young koala sleeps on its mother's back.

koalas

An alligator floats in the water.

alligator

A hippopotamus naps in the sun.

hippopotamus

A sleepy lion
opens wide.

lion

A cheetah lies in a soft clump of grass.

cheetah

A rhinoceros rests in the shade.

rhinoceros

A fox curls up for a snooze.

fox

Four flamingos tuck their heads under their wings.

flamingos

A young giraffe folds its long legs.

Two tigers stretch out by a log.

A young zebra
lies still.

zebra

An ibex rests its head on its hooves.

ibex

Zoo animals can sleep almost anywhere.
Can you?

polar bear

Where can I find...

an alligator? ....pages 6–7
a cheetah? ....pages 12–13
flamingos? ....pages 18–19
a fox? ....pages 16–17
a giraffe? ....pages 20–21
a hippopotamus? ....pages 8–9
an ibex? ....pages 26–27
koalas? ....pages 4–5
a lion? ....pages 10–11, 31
an orangutan? ....page 3
a panda? ....page 1
a polar bear? ....page 29
a rhinoceros? ....pages 14–15
tigers? ....pages 22–23
a zebra? ....pages 24–25

lion

Caroline Arnold has written more than one hundred books for children. Many of the books are about animals. Caroline lives with her husband in Los Angeles, California.

Richard Hewett worked for magazines before he discovered children's books. He, too, has created many books about animals. Richard lives with his wife in Los Angeles, California.

Text copyright © 1999 by Caroline Arnold
Photographs copyright © 1999 by Richard R. Hewett
Additional photographs courtesy of: © Caroline Arnold, p. 9; © Arthur Arnold, p. 1

All rights reserved. International copyright secured. No part of this book may be reproduced, stored in a retrieval system, or transmitted in any form or by any means, electronic, mechanical, photocopying, recording, or otherwise, without the prior written permission of Carolrhoda Books, Inc., except for the inclusion of brief quotations in an acknowledged review.

This book is available in two bindings:
ISBN 1-57505-290-3 (lib. bdg.)
ISBN 1-57505-393-4 (trade bdg.)

Carolrhoda Books, Inc., c/o The Lerner Publishing Group
241 First Avenue North, Minneapolis, MN 55401 U.S.A.

Website address: www.lernerbooks.com

Library of Congress Cataloging-in-Publication Data

Arnold, Caroline.
   Sleepytime for zoo animals / by Caroline Arnold ; photographs by Richard Hewett.
      p.   cm.
   Includes index.
   Summary: Describes how and where zoo animals sleep.
   ISBN 1-57505-290-3 (lib. bdg. : alk. paper)
   1. Zoo animals—Behavior—Juvenile literature. 2. Sleep behavior in animals—Juvenile literature. [1. Zoo animals 2. Sleep.] I. Hewett, Richard, ill. II. Title.
QL77.5.A85   1999
636.088'9—dc21   98-24377

Manufactured in the United States of America
1 2 3 4 5 6 – JR – 04 03 02 01 00 99